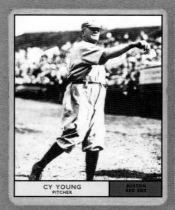

CY YOUNG
PITCHER

BOSTON
RED SOX

DOM DiMAGGIO
CENTER FIELDER

BOSTON
RED SOX

THE STORY OF THE BOSTON RED SOX

Published by Creative Paperbacks
P.O. Box 227, Mankato, Minnesota 56002
Creative Paperbacks is an imprint of The Creative Company
www.thecreativecompany.us

Design and production by Blue Design
Art direction by Rita Marshall
Printed by Corporate Graphics in the United States of America

Photographs by Corbis (Bettmann), Getty Images (APA, Al Bello, Bruce Bennett Studios, Diamond Images, Steve Dunwell, Elsa, Focus on Sport, FPG, Jeff Gross, Otto Greule Jr./Allsport, Andy Hayt, Carl Iwasaki/Time & Life Pictures, G. Newman Lowrance, Brad Mangin/MLB Photos, National Baseball Hall of Fame Library/MLB Photos, Gary Newkirk, Rich Pilling/MLB Photos, Photo File, Jim Rogash, Mark Rucker/Transcendental Graphics, Joseph Scherschel/Time & Life Pictures, Ezra Shaw, Brian Snyder-Pool, Rick Stewart, Ron Vesely/MLB Photos)

The Library of Congress has cataloged the hardcover edition as follows:

Goodman, Michael E.
The story of the Boston Red Sox / by Michael E. Goodman.
p. cm. — (Baseball: the great American game)
Includes index.
Summary: The history of the Boston Red Sox professional baseball team from its inaugural 1901 season to today, spotlighting the team's greatest players and most memorable moments.
ISBN 978-1-60818-034-9 (hardcover)
ISBN 978-0-89812-632-7 (pbk)
1. Boston Red Sox (Baseball team)—History—Juvenile literature. I. Title. II. Series.

GV875.B62G68 2011
796.357'640974461—dc22   2010023566

CPSIA: 031212 PO1556

9 8 7 6 5 4 3 2

Page 3: Third baseman Wade Boggs
Page 4: Center fielder Jacoby Ellsbury

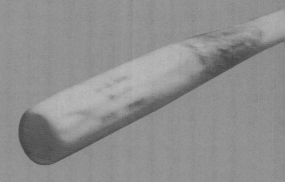

BASEBALL: THE GREAT AMERICAN GAME

THE STORY OF THE BOSTON RED SOX

Michael E. Goodman

CREATIVE
PAPER BACKS

CONTENTS

SETTLING IN NEW ENGLAND

In 1630, a group of devoutly religious men and women called Puritans left their homes near the town of Boston in eastern England and sailed across the Atlantic Ocean to start new lives in New England. They settled on a hilly peninsula fed by a freshwater spring and called the town Boston, after their old home. The Puritans believed strongly in education, and they built America's first public schools, libraries, and college, which was named after Puritan minister John Harvard. Even today, Boston remains a center of education and culture in the United States.

Boston is also a major hub for professional sports in America, and New Englanders fiercely root for basketball's Celtics, football's Patriots, and hockey's Bruins. But the club that receives their greatest devotion is the Boston Red Sox, a member of Major League Baseball's American League (AL) since 1901. The team actually began as the Pilgrims and wore blue socks. Then, before the 1908 season, owner John Taylor decided to liven things up by changing the stockings to bright red, leading local newspapers to dub the team the "Red Sox."

Between pro baseball, basketball, and football, sports fans in Boston and throughout New England celebrated six world championships from 2001 to 2008.

PITCHER · CY YOUNG

Early in the career of Denton True Young, his fastball blew by so many hitters that fans and teammates began to call him "Cyclone." Over time, the nickname was shortened to "Cy." During his 22-year career, 8 years of which were spent with the Red Sox, Young started more than 800 games and pitched more than 7,000 innings without suffering a serious injury.

CY YOUNG
PITCHER

BOSTON
RED SOX

His major-league record of 511 career victories is nearly 100 more than the second-best total. His total of 316 losses is also a longstanding record. Today, baseball annually honors the best pitcher in each league with the Cy Young Award.

STATS

Red Sox seasons: 1901–08

Height: 6-foot-2

Weight: 210

- **5 seasons of 30 or more wins**

- **749 complete games (most all-time)**

- **2,803 career strikeouts**

- **Baseball Hall of Fame inductee (1937)**

BILL DINNEEN

The Boston franchise rose quickly to the top of the AL, winning pennants in both 1903 and 1904. The club featured outstanding pitching, highlighted by Denton "Cy" Young—baseball's all-time winningest pitcher—and stocky right-hander Bill Dinneen. The top hitting star was outfielder Buck Freeman, whose 13 home runs and 104 runs batted in (RBI) in 1903 were both league bests.

The 1903 club earned a special place in baseball history. After winning the AL title, it took on the National League (NL) champion Pittsburgh Pirates in a best-of-nine "World Series." The Pilgrims lost three of the first four contests, then won the next four games to claim baseball's first world championship. Some observers said the key to the Pilgrims' victory was not a hitter or pitcher, but a song sung over and over by some of Boston's loudest fans. The lyrics made fun of several Pirates and seemed to rattle them. "It sort of got on your nerves after a while," said one Pittsburgh player. The Pilgrims won the AL pennant again in 1904 but didn't play in a World Series that year because the NL's New York Giants refused to take on any team of "inferior" American Leaguers.

Over the next few years, Taylor initiated many changes within his club, starting with its new name in 1908. Taylor also traded away many of the team's best players and replaced them with young, inexpensive talent. He used some of the money he saved to purchase land in Boston's Fenway region for a new stadium that would open in 1912. Luckily for Red Sox fans, several of the young players that Taylor brought in would become stars in the new Fenway Park, including fireballing pitcher "Smoky" Joe Wood and smooth-swinging center fielder Tris Speaker.

Wood simply overpowered batters with his blistering fastball. Once, legendary pitcher Walter Johnson—famous for his own blazing "heater"—was asked if he could throw harder than the Red Sox hurler. "Listen, my friend," Johnson replied. "No man alive can throw harder than Smoky Joe Wood."

Speaker, meanwhile, was the team's fielding and hitting leader. Incredibly fast and blessed with a cannon of an arm, Speaker played very shallow in center. "I learned early that I could save more games by cutting off singles hit over the infield than I would lose by having an occasional extra-base hit go over my head," he explained. On offense, Speaker's speed and power anchored a lineup that scored runs in bunches.

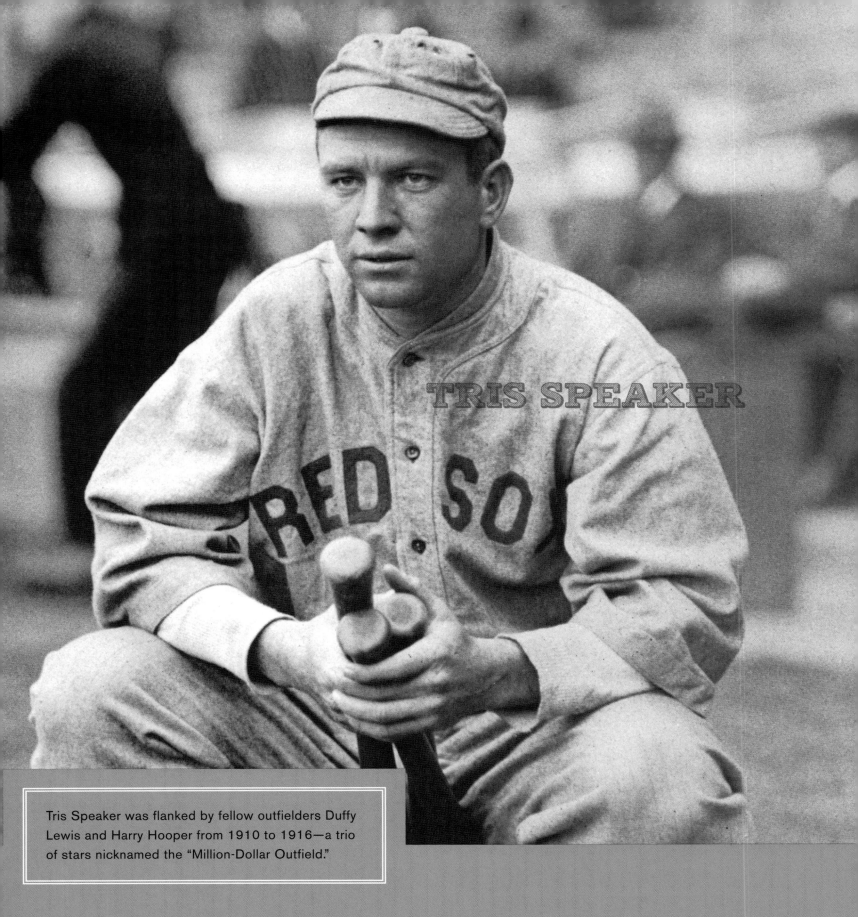

TRIS SPEAKER

Tris Speaker was flanked by fellow outfielders Duffy Lewis and Harry Hooper from 1910 to 1916—a trio of stars nicknamed the "Million-Dollar Outfield."

JOE WOOD

THE DUEL

On September 6, 1912, two of the hardest-throwing pitchers in baseball history—Boston's Smoky Joe Wood and the Washington Senators' Walter Johnson—faced off in Fenway Park. A standing-room-only crowd pushed and shoved to get a good view of the duel, which was being billed as "The War of 1912." The duel had a special significance. Earlier in the season, Johnson had set a league record by winning 16 straight games, and Wood was now riding a 13-win streak that Johnson hoped to stop. Both pitchers were nearly unhittable for the first five innings, mowing down batter after batter. The score stood 0–0 with two outs in the bottom of the

sixth. Then, Boston center fielder Tris Speaker slapped a ground-rule double to left off Johnson, and center fielder Duffy Lewis followed with a soft looper to right that barely dropped in, allowing Speaker to race home. That was all the support Wood needed. He quickly recorded the final nine outs for the 1–0 shutout victory. Wood would win his next two starts also, tying Johnson's record. "Some games deserve to be remembered by the entire baseball community for all time," wrote baseball historian Emil Rothe. "The Johnson–Wood contest was one of those."

CATCHER · JASON VARITEK

A natural leader, Varitek was named team captain in 2004, becoming only the third in Red Sox history. A fiery competitor, the big catcher was known for his constant hustle. He was also known for a scuffle with New York Yankees slugger Alex Rodriguez at home plate in 2004, when Rodriguez threatened a Red Sox pitcher after being hit by a pitch. Varitek's willingness to stand up for his pitcher endeared him to fans and teammates alike. One of the better hitting catchers in the major leagues, the switch-hitting Varitek was a long-ball threat from either side of the plate.

JASON VARITEK
CATCHER

BOSTON
RED SOX

STATS

Red Sox seasons: 1997–present

Height: 6-foot-2

Weight: 230

- **2005 Gold Glove winner**

- **182 career HR**

- **3-time All-Star**

- **Career-best 25 HR in 2003**

FIRST BASEMAN · MO VAUGHN

Vaughn was one of the most feared hitters in baseball during the 1990s, and his trademark high-rising home runs made him a favorite among Red Sox fans. He was also an RBI threat. "When I step up to the plate, I consider a man on first to already be in scoring position," Vaughn once boasted. Known as "The Hit Dog," the left-handed slugger always stood close to the plate with his arms holding the bat high overhead. Leaning over the plate, Vaughn dared pitchers to throw inside, where his quick wrists and incredible strength turned fastballs into long balls.

MO VAUGHN
FIRST BASEMAN

BOSTON
RED SOX

STATS

Red Sox seasons: 1991–98

Height: 6-foot-1

Weight: 230

- **1995 AL MVP**

- **3-time All-Star**

- **1,064 career RBI**

- **Career-best 44 HR in 1996**

In 1912, the two stars led Boston to another AL pennant. Wood had a near-perfect season, going 34–5 with 10 shutouts, and Speaker earned the league's Most Valuable Player (MVP) award by hitting .383 while scoring 136 runs and stealing 52 bases. In the World Series against the Giants, Wood notched three victories, and Speaker and fellow outfielder Harry Hooper provided key hits to propel Boston to its second championship.

THE BABE, HERE AND GONE

I n 1914, the Red Sox signed a 19-year-old pitcher who would have a major impact on franchise history—in ways both positive and negative. That pitcher was stocky left-hander George Herman "Babe" Ruth. By 1916, Ruth was a 20-game winner and one of the best hurlers in the league. But what really impressed fans was Ruth's ability to hit a baseball hard and far, and he often played in the field between pitching starts. Led by Ruth's arm and bat, the Red Sox became a dominant team, winning world championships in 1915, 1916, and 1918. Off the field, however, the Babe caused problems in Boston. He constantly squabbled with team management over money, and his desire to play in the outfield rather than pitch irritated his teammates.

The prospect of giving Ruth a big raise, coupled with Red Sox owner Harry Frazee's personal debts, prompted Frazee to sell the Babe to the New York Yankees in 1920 for $125,000. A popular legend has it that, upon

BABE RUTH

Nicknamed "The Bambino" and "The Sultan of Swat,"
Babe Ruth slugged 29 homers (a new personal high)
in 1919, his farewell season with the Sox.

SECOND BASEMAN · BOBBY DOERR

A teenage phenom, Doerr was in the majors and starting for the Red Sox at age 19. In his major-league debut, Doerr lashed the first 3 of what would be 2,000 hits in a stellar 14-year career. A superb fielder, Doerr once handled 414 straight chances without an error, a league record at the time. At the plate, the solidly built Doerr displayed uncommon pop for a middle infielder but still hit for a high average. Perhaps Doerr's most marked characteristic was his gentlemanly style of play. During his 14 seasons, he was never ejected from a game.

STATS

Red Sox seasons: 1937–44, 1946–51

Height: 5-foot-11

Weight: 180

- 9-time All-Star
- 223 career HR
- 6 seasons with 100 or more RBI
- Baseball Hall of Fame inductee (1986)

BOBBY DOERR
SECOND BASEMAN

BOSTON
RED SOX

leaving Boston, Ruth put a curse on the Sox to make sure they would never win a World Series without him. Whether it was magic or myth, the "Curse of the Bambino" seemed to haunt the Red Sox for decades.

Frazee made several other bad decisions in the early 1920s, trading or selling off top players, including shortstop Everett Scott and pitcher Carl Mays. The Red Sox's few remaining stars, such as hard-hitting outfielder Earl Webb and sidearm pitcher Howard Ehmke, were not able to keep the team in contention. Boston fell to the bottom half of the AL standings and stayed there for more than a decade.

The team's fortunes finally started to turn around in the mid-1930s after Thomas Yawkey purchased the team. Committed to improving the downtrodden Sox, Yawkey spent freely to obtain top stars, such as shortstop Joe Cronin (who would double as player/manager) and two future Hall-of-Famers—slugging first baseman Jimmie Foxx and strikeout king Lefty Grove. Yawkey also built up the team's "farm" system, which produced such standouts as steady-hitting second baseman Bobby Doerr and outfielder Ted Williams.

The tall, skinny Williams didn't look like much when he came to the Red Sox in 1939, but his outstanding play quickly earned him the nickname "The Splendid Splinter." Williams combined keen vision, knowledge of the strike zone, and perhaps the most graceful left-handed swing the game had ever seen to produce incredible offensive numbers. In 1941, Williams posted a .406 batting average, making him still the most recent player to hit .400 or better for a season. By the end of his career, Williams had slugged 521 home runs and owned a .344 lifetime average. "All I want out of life," he once said, "is that when I walk down the street, folks will say, 'there goes the greatest hitter who ever lived.'"

In the early '40s, Williams and several of Boston's other stars left the game to serve their country in World War II. In 1946, after the war ended, they returned and led Boston to the AL pennant. In addition to Williams and Doerr, the team featured swift center fielder Dom DiMaggio, slick-fielding shortstop Johnny Pesky, and hard-throwing pitcher Dave "Boo" Ferriss. In the World Series, the Red Sox faced the St. Louis Cardinals. The series went a full seven games, but the Cardinals prevailed, winning 4–3 in the final contest.

Boston would not reach the playoffs for the rest of the 1940s and '50s. Although always a good team, the Red Sox consistently finished behind the great Yankees clubs of the time, a fact that added fuel to the already intense

THIRD BASEMAN · WADE BOGGS

A student of hitting technique, Boggs was perhaps the best two-strike hitter who ever lived. He patiently took pitches and fouled off others, sizing up the pitcher's delivery with each throw, before calmly slashing a line drive into Fenway's outfield. An eight-time All-Star with the Sox, Boggs was a firm believer in routine. He ate chicken before every game and had a pregame regimen of drills and exercises from which he never strayed. Only an adequate fielder when he arrived in the big leagues, Boggs tirelessly worked on his defense until he eventually became a two-time Gold Glove winner.

WADE BOGGS
THIRD BASEMAN

BOSTON
RED SOX

STATS

Red Sox seasons: 1982–92

Height: 6-foot-2

Weight: 197

- **.328 career BA**

- **3,010 career hits**

- **1,513 career runs scored**

- **Baseball Hall of Fame inductee (2005)**

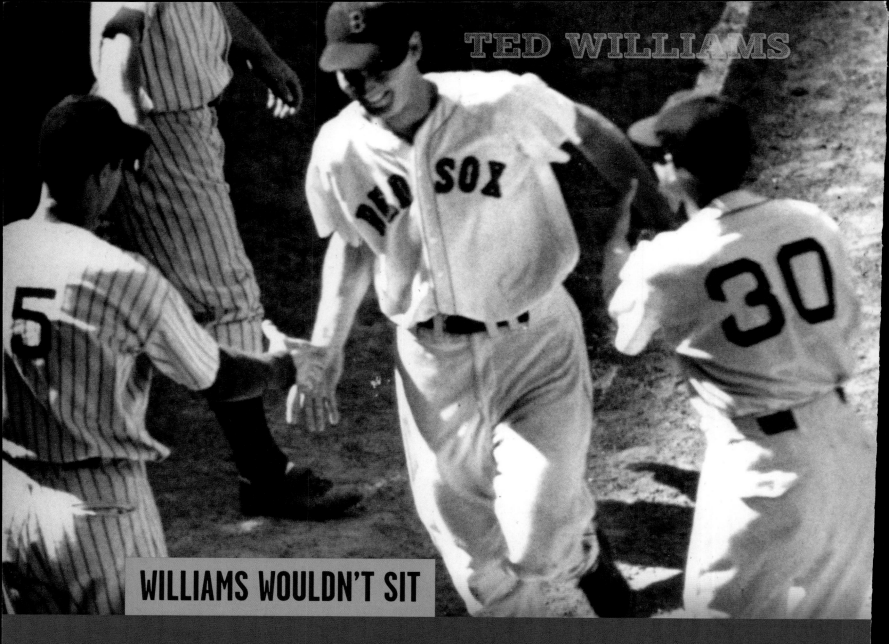

WILLIAMS WOULDN'T SIT

RED SOX

With one week remaining in the 1941 season, Boston left fielder Ted Williams was on the verge of making baseball history. His batting average stood at a remarkable .406. Only 7 other players in the 20th century had broken the .400 barrier, and Williams was poised to be number 8. Boston manager Joe Cronin suggested that Williams sit out the rest of the season. "You don't want to risk that .400 average by making a lot of outs. Just sit down," advised Cronin. But Williams felt he must keep playing to truly earn his .400. Over the next few games, Williams's average did indeed drop,

falling to .39955 with one day remaining in the season. That number rounded off to an even .400—if Williams sat down then. One more at bat ending in an out would drop the average to .399. Once again, Williams refused to stay on the bench. He played both ends of a last-day doubleheader, smacking six hits in eight at bats to raise his average to a solid .406. No player since 1941 has joined Williams in the exclusive .400 club. By refusing to sit down and take the easy route, the Splendid Splinter certainly earned his place in history.

East Coast rivalry. "We'd win 80 games, they would win 90. We'd win 90 games, they would win 100," explained Boston catcher Sammy White. "No matter what we did, the Yankees always seemed to do just a little bit more."

YAZ CONQUERS THE MONSTER

T he year after Williams retired in 1960, another power-hitting left fielder arrived in Fenway Park. Carl Yastrzemski, known to fans simply as "Yaz," brought a fiercely competitive spirit to the game. "When I came up, people expected me to be the next Williams," said Yastrzemski. "I knew there was only one Ted Williams, but I was going to give them everything Carl Yastrzemski had." That confident attitude, along with a smooth left-handed stroke, helped Yaz win three AL batting titles. A superb fielder as well, Yaz knew every angle, bump, and carom that the "Green Monster"—Fenway's 37-foot-high left-field wall—could produce.

Despite Yastrzemski's prowess, the Red Sox struggled through the mid-1960s. Then, in 1967, the Sox caught fire. Fueled by Yaz's Triple Crown season (he led the AL in homers, RBI, and batting average), the Red Sox rocketed to the top of the league. Other standouts on that pennant-winning club were graceful first baseman George Scott, slugging outfielder Tony Conigliaro, and control pitcher Jim Lonborg. Unfortunately, the season ended badly, with the Sox losing a tense seven-game World Series to the Cardinals.

In 1969, Major League Baseball split each of the two leagues into divisions, and in 1975, the Red Sox stormed to their first AL Eastern Division title. Yaz remained the team's heart and soul, but Boston had also bolstered its lineup with young stars such as New Hampshire-born catcher Carlton Fisk and multitalented outfielders Jim Rice, Fred Lynn, and Dwight Evans. In the playoffs, the Red Sox knocked off the Oakland A's in the AL Championship Series (ALCS) and then met the Cincinnati Reds in the World Series. The series was filled with high drama, with Game 6 ending on a memorable walk-off home run by Fisk and Game 7 going down to the ninth inning before the Reds pushed across the winning run.

CARL YASTRZEMSKI

Carl Yastrzemski's 23 seasons in Boston set a major-league record; only one other player (Baltimore Orioles great Brooks Robinson) had such a long career with a single team.

SHORTSTOP · NOMAR GARCIAPARRA

Garciaparra's unusual first name is actually his father's name, Ramon, spelled backwards. A hard swinger with pop in his bat, the California native belted 30 home runs during his first full season in the majors. Garciaparra also wowed fans with his strong throwing arm. Perhaps the trait that most endeared him to Red Sox fans, though, was his constant hustle. Whether beating out an infield hit or ranging deep in the hole to snare a tough grounder, Garciaparra always gave his all. "You go out there and play hard and make plays," he explained. "That's what playing for this team is about."

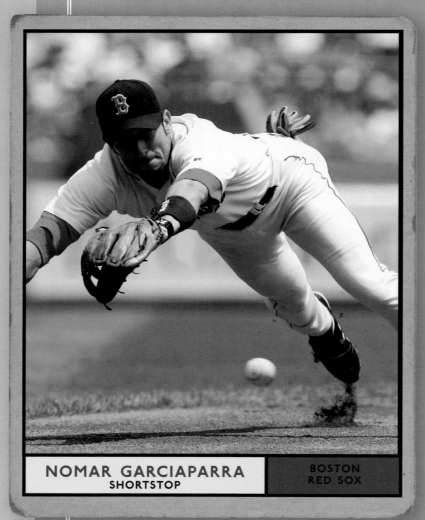

NOMAR GARCIAPARRA
SHORTSTOP

BOSTON
RED SOX

STATS

Red Sox seasons: 1996–2004

Height: 6 feet

Weight: 190

- **1997 AL Rookie of the Year**

- **6-time All-Star**

- **2-time AL batting champ**

- **7 seasons with 20 or more HR**

Boston contended for the AL East title again in 1978. After finishing
the regular season tied with the Yankees, the Sox took on the Yanks in
a one-game playoff at Fenway Park. Late in the game, light-hitting New
York shortstop Bucky Dent popped a fly ball over the Green Monster for
a three-run homer to give the Yankees a lead they would not relinquish.
Most Boston fans believed the Curse of the Bambino had struck again.

By the mid-1980s, a new group of stars was shining in Fenway Park,
including hit-machine third baseman Wade Boggs, smooth-swinging
left fielder Mike Greenwell, and flamethrowing pitcher Roger Clemens.
Boggs was not a power hitter, but his uncanny ability to spray line drives

LEFT FIELDER · TED WILLIAMS

Arguably the greatest hitter who ever lived, Williams's keen eyesight allowed him to "pick out the stitches" on the ball as it was delivered. His greatness was on full display during his two Triple Crown seasons in 1942 and 1947, when he led the league in homers, RBI, and batting average. Despite losing nearly five years of his career to military service in two wars, Williams's career offensive totals rank among the game's all-time greats. "Ted Williams gave baseball some of its best seasons, and he gave his own best seasons to his country," said president George W. Bush after Williams passed away in 2002.

TED WILLIAMS
LEFT FIELDER

BOSTON
RED SOX

STATS

Red Sox seasons: 1939–42, 1946–60

Height: 6-foot-3

Weight: 205

- **17-time All-Star**
- **521 career HR**
- **.344 lifetime BA**
- **Baseball Hall of Fame inductee (1966)**

CARLTON FISK

FISK WAVES IT FAIR

Game-winning home runs are always exciting, but game-winning home runs in extra innings in the World Series instantly become part of baseball history. Red Sox catcher Carlton Fisk provided one of the game's most dramatic moments when he faced the Cincinnati Reds' Pat Darcy in Game 6 of the 1975 World Series. It was the 12th inning, and the score was knotted 6–6 when Fisk launched a Darcy pitch high and deep down the left-field line at Fenway Park. At first, it looked as if the ball would hook foul, but Fisk, watching the flight of the ball from home plate, jumped and waved his arms to his right, desperately willing the ball fair. As Red Sox fans held their breath, the ball ricocheted off the foul pole for a home run. Two inches farther left, and it would have just been a strike. Fisk's blast won the game and sent the series to a deciding seventh contest the next night. The Reds ended up winning Game 7 and the series, but more people remember only Fisk's heroic home run and willful wave, a moment that *TV Guide* claimed in 1998 was "the greatest moment in the history of sports television."

RED SOX

all over the field made him equally as dangerous. During his career in Boston, Boggs would capture five AL batting titles. Clemens gave Boston what it had lacked for years—a power pitching ace. "The Rocket" controlled the plate with his blazing fastball. "Roger is a good guy," said Red Sox catcher Rich Gedman, "but when he is pitching, hitters are not just opponents, they are the enemy."

In 1986, Clemens won 24 games, and Boggs hit .357 to lead Boston to the AL East crown. After advancing to the World Series with an ALCS win over the California Angels, Boston jumped out to a three-games-to-two lead over the New York Mets. In Game 6 in New York, the Sox held a 5–3 lead with 2 outs in the bottom of the 10th inning; only 1 out separated them from their first championship since 1918. Then, disaster struck: three Mets singles, a wild pitch, and a fielding error by Boston first baseman Bill Buckner combined to give the Mets three runs and the victory. In Game 7, the Mets finished off the reeling Sox, 8–5, to win the series. "This game breaks your heart," said Evans. "I've been around a long time, but I've never seen anything like this."

ENDING THE CURSE

ith the help of Boggs, Clemens, and Greenwell, the Red Sox remained a contender for the rest of the 1980s, battling with the Toronto Blue Jays for supremacy in the AL East. In both 1988 and 1990, Boston captured division titles but lost in the ALCS to mighty Oakland. The club then went into a downward spin, finishing with losing records from 1992 to 1994.

The Red Sox bounced back in 1995, however, led by burly first baseman Mo Vaughn, whose powerful left-handed swing struck terror into the hearts of opposing pitchers. In 1995, Vaughn smashed 39 homers and drove in 126 runs—numbers that both led the Sox to another AL East title and earned the first baseman the AL MVP award. But even with Vaughn wreaking havoc on the ball, the Sox were unable to reach the World Series again. Boggs had departed, Clemens and Vaughn soon left as free agents, and Boston was again in rebuilding mode.

By 2002, the Red Sox began to take on a new look. Hard-hitting shortstop Nomar Garciaparra, slugging outfielder Manny Ramirez,

CENTER FIELDER · DOM DiMAGGIO

Known as the "Little Professor" because of his thick glasses and small stature, DiMaggio played in the shadow of his more famous teammate, Ted Williams, and his brother, New York Yankees star Joe DiMaggio. Quiet and unassuming, Dom DiMaggio was a great player in his own right. Swift and sure-handed, he effortlessly tracked down rockets that appeared certain to be hits. Red Sox fans joked that DiMaggio had to play both center and left field to cover for the slow-footed Williams. At the plate, DiMaggio was a superb leadoff hitter and base runner who once put together a 34-game hitting streak.

DOM DiMAGGIO
CENTER FIELDER

BOSTON
RED SOX

STATS

Red Sox seasons: 1940–42, 1946–53

Height: 5-foot-9

Weight: 168

- 7-time All-Star

- .298 career BA

- 1,680 career hits

- 2-time AL leader in runs scored

PEDRO MARTINEZ

and fiery pitcher Pedro Martinez formed the nucleus of the team.
Garciaparra had great range in the field and could hit for both power and
a high average. He also displayed a flair for making big, game-altering
plays. Ramirez came to Boston as a free agent from the Cleveland
Indians. He excelled at hitting with runners on base, consistently
ranking among the league's RBI leaders. Martinez was small in stature
(5-foot-11 and 170 pounds) but possessed a hard-breaking slider and
brought a confident swagger to the mound.

In 2003, the Red Sox made it to the postseason before the Curse of the
Bambino struck again. In Game 7 of the ALCS between the Sox and the

JONATHAN PAPELBON

Yankees, New York rallied to tie the contest when Boston manager Grady Little left a tiring Martinez on the mound too long. Then, in the bottom of the 11th inning, third baseman Aaron Boone—a player not known for his power—hit a walk-off home run to win the game and the series for New York. For Sox fans, the moment was eerily reminiscent of Bucky Dent's devastating homer in 1978. Boston sportswriter Bill Simmons spoke for many Sox fans when he wrote, "Does any of this make sense? Of course not. The Red Sox have driven me insane."

Prior to the 2004 campaign, Boston welcomed a new manager, Terry Francona, and a new pitching star, outspoken right-hander Curt Schilling. The club also said goodbye to Garciaparra, whose frequent injuries and bickering with team management led to his being traded at midseason to the Chicago Cubs. Luckily, Ramirez and designated hitter David Ortiz, lovingly called "Big Papi" by Red Sox fans, assumed leadership of Boston's offense and led the

AMERICAN LEAGUE

P		1 2 3 4 5 6 7 8 9	H
25	PHILA.	2 0 0 1 0	7
33	BOSTON	2 0 0 1 2	6
26	WASH.	0 0 0 0 1	
21	NEW YORK	2 0 0 3 0	

FENWAY PARK

BALL (H) STRIKE

OUT (E) AT BAT

AMERICAN LEAGUE

P		1 2 3 4 5 6 7 8 9 10
17	CHICAGO	
44	ST. LOUIS	
19	DETROIT	
23	CLEVE.	

NATIONAL LEAGUE

	IN R		IN R
BOSTON	5 9	ST. LOUIS	1 0
PHILA.	1	CHICAGO	0
NEW YORK	1 0	CINN.	
BROOK.	1	PITTS.	

HERE TO-MORROW
WASH.

Pleasant Moments

PM

THE GREEN MONSTER

Fenway Park's tall left-field wall has been a part of the stadium since it opened in 1912. The "Green Monster," as it has come to be known, looms a mere 310 feet from home plate and stands 37 feet tall. What many people don't know is that at one time, the Green Monster wasn't green, and it wasn't such a monstrosity. Prior to 1934, the fence stood only 25 feet high, and before 1947, the fence wasn't green but was instead covered with advertisements. The Red Sox chose to raise the fence and put netting on top of it to protect the windows of buildings on Landsdowne Street from home run balls.

The dark green paint first appeared during a stadium renovation. The tall wall has intrigued fans and players alike for decades and in some cases has confused its first-time viewers. When rookie pitcher Bill Lee joined the team in 1969, a veteran asked him if he'd ever seen Fenway Park. Lee had not, so the veteran walked him out on the field and asked him what he thought of the Green Monster. The inexperienced pitcher gawked at the wall, then turned to the veteran and asked, "Do they leave that up during the game?"

RIGHT FIELDER · DWIGHT EVANS

One of the greatest right fielders of any era, "Dewey," as he was known, could field any hit in his direction and come up throwing. Base runners seldom tried to take an extra base on his arm. Evans also had a knack for making dramatic catches. His leaping grab of a would-be home run late in Game 6 of the 1975 World Series saved the game, if not the series, for the Red Sox. Over his 19 seasons in Boston, Red Sox fans grew to rely on the durable Evans's remarkable productivity. He hit 20 or more home runs in 11 seasons.

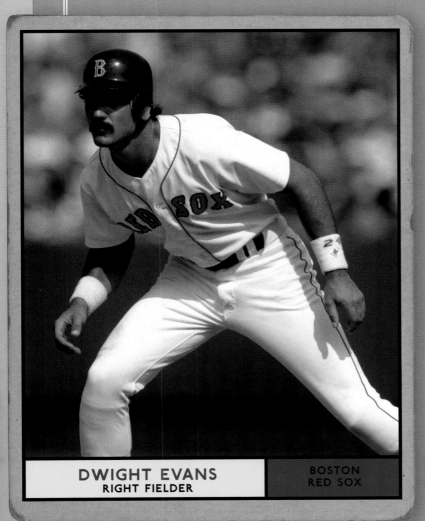

DWIGHT EVANS
RIGHT FIELDER

BOSTON
RED SOX

STATS

Red Sox seasons: 1972–90

Height: 6-foot-2

Weight: 205

- **3-time All-Star**

- **8-time Gold Glove winner**

- **385 career HR**

- **2,446 career hits**

MANAGER · JOE CRONIN

The winningest manager in Red Sox history, Cronin guided Boston to 1,071 victories during his 13 seasons at the helm. Cronin was one of the last player/managers in the major leagues. An excellent shortstop, he carried a .301 lifetime batting average. Cronin came to the Red Sox in 1935, when team owner Tom Yawkey purchased him from the Washington Senators for the then-astronomical figure of $225,000. After retiring as manager of the Red Sox in 1947, Cronin served as the team's general manager before going on to become the first former player to be named a league president.

JOE CRONIN
MANAGER

BOSTON
RED SOX

STATS

Red Sox seasons as manager:
1935–47

Managerial record: 1,236–1,055

AL pennants: 1933, 1946

Baseball Hall of Fame inductee
(1956)

club to another playoff berth, this time as the AL Wild Card team.

After quickly dispatching the Anaheim Angels in the AL Division Series (ALDS), the Red Sox again faced the Yankees in the ALCS. New York started fast, winning the first three games of the series. Then the Red Sox staged a miraculous comeback, winning both Games 4 and 5 in extra innings on dramatic Ortiz homers. Inspired by the big slugger's exploits and boosted by their fans' frenzied support, the Sox then rolled to victories in Games 6 and 7 at Yankee Stadium, becoming the first team ever to come back from a three-games-to-zero deficit to win a playoff series.

Riding high, the Red Sox faced another old nemesis in the World Series—the St. Louis Cardinals. But this time there would be no

suspense. Boston crushed the Cardinals in four straight games to capture its first world championship since 1918 and officially end the Curse of the Bambino. "This [victory] is for Ted Williams, Yaz, and all the other great players who made this franchise what it is today," said an emotional Schilling. "We are all proud to wear this uniform."

DAVID ORTIZ

STAYING ON TOP

Red Sox fans had waited 86 years to celebrate a World Series victory, but they were already impatient for another championship. With such high expectations, the next two seasons were disappointments in Boston. The Red Sox made the playoffs as the AL Wild Card in 2005 but lost to the Chicago White Sox in the ALDS. Then, in 2006, Boston slipped out of the postseason picture with an 86–76 record.

Hopes for a rebound in 2007 increased when the Red Sox added sensational Japanese hurler Daisuke Matsuzaka to a pitching staff that already featured hard-throwing starter Josh Beckett, knuckleballer Tim Wakefield, and star closer Jonathan Papelbon. The team also had two rookie fielding stars in gritty second baseman Dustin Pedroia and speedy outfielder Jacoby Ellsbury. "I'm very excited," said Boston general manager Theo Epstein. "This has a chance to be a pretty special club."

Epstein's words proved prophetic. With Pedroia setting the table with timely hitting and Ortiz, steady third baseman Mike Lowell, and strapping first baseman Kevin Youkilis driving in runs, the Sox opened

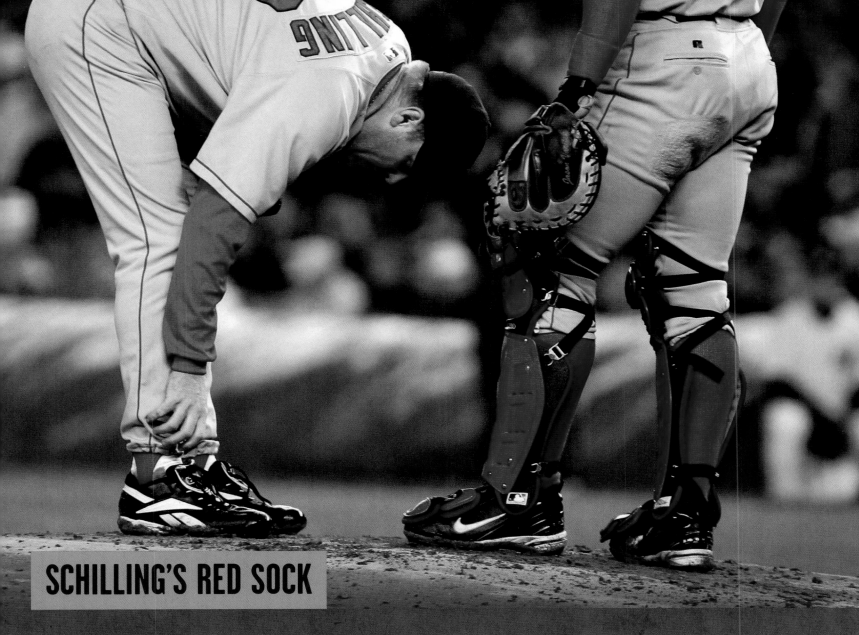

SCHILLING'S RED SOCK

Things did not look good for the Red Sox during the 2004 ALCS. Down three games to two against their bitter rivals, the Yankees, the Sox sent Curt Schilling to the mound for Game 6. Normally one of the game's best hurlers, Schilling had torn a tendon in his ankle prior to the series, and it hampered his delivery. Pitching against the Yankees in Game 1, he was roughed up for six runs in three innings. Before Game 6, team doctors tried to secure the injured tendon by stitching it to Schilling's skin. In obvious pain, Schilling took the mound and gutted out seven strong innings. Midway through his performance, Schilling's stitches ruptured, and blood soaked through his uniform sock. Schilling's courageous pitching inspired fans and teammates alike, and the Sox went on to defeat the Yankees 4–2. Just five days later, a re-stitched Schilling took the mound again, this time facing the Cardinals in Game 2 of the World Series. He performed masterfully, getting the win while giving up only one run in six innings. Many Red Sox fans cited Schilling's iron-willed feats as the key to Boston's stunning postseason success that year.

RED SOX

JOHNNY PESKY

THE PESKY POLE

Shortstop Johnny Pesky was one of the all-time greatest Red Sox players. He was a superb fielder, and his lifetime .307 batting average is a testament to his hitting skill, but at 5-foot-9 and 165 pounds, he was never known as a long-ball threat. During his 7 and a half seasons in Boston during the 1940s and '50s, Pesky slugged just 14 home runs, and only 6 of them were hit at Fenway Park. On the rare occasion when Pesky did hit a homer in Fenway, his "shots" just barely slipped over the 3-foot-tall right-field fence directly next to the foul pole—a mere 302 feet away from home plate. While broadcasting a Red Sox game decades later, former Red Sox pitcher Mel Parnell witnessed someone else imitating Pesky's unusual style of banking a homer off the right-field foul pole. Parnell jokingly dubbed the tall yellow marker the "Pesky Pole," in honor of his former teammate. The nickname stuck, memorializing both Johnny Pesky and his pole. Today, more than 50 years after Pesky hit his last home run, a hitter who hooks a ball around the right-field foul pole in Fenway Park is said to have "wrapped one around the Pesky Pole."

an early season lead in the AL East. Beckett dominated opponents with his mixture of fastballs and sliders, finishing the year at 20–7 and leading Boston to another division title. Then the Red Sox outfought the Angels and the Cleveland Indians in the postseason to reach the World Series, this time versus the upstart NL champs, the Colorado Rockies.

As in 2004, the World Series was not nearly as exciting as the AL playoffs. Although Colorado came into the "Fall Classic" red-hot—having won 21 of its previous 22 games, including 7 straight postseason contests—Boston quickly swept the Rockies in 4 straight games, making the Red Sox champs for the second time in 4 years. Francona was particularly impressed with Beckett's performance in the postseason. "He's maturing right in front of our eyes," the Boston skipper said. "It seems like every game, he wants to make more of a name for himself."

The Sox came close to repeating in 2008 when they reached the playoffs as a Wild Card team but fell short against the Tampa Bay Rays in an exciting seven-game ALCS. Pedroia led the way, earning a Gold Glove award for his fielding and the AL MVP award for his superb all-around play. As had become commonplace for the Red Sox, the

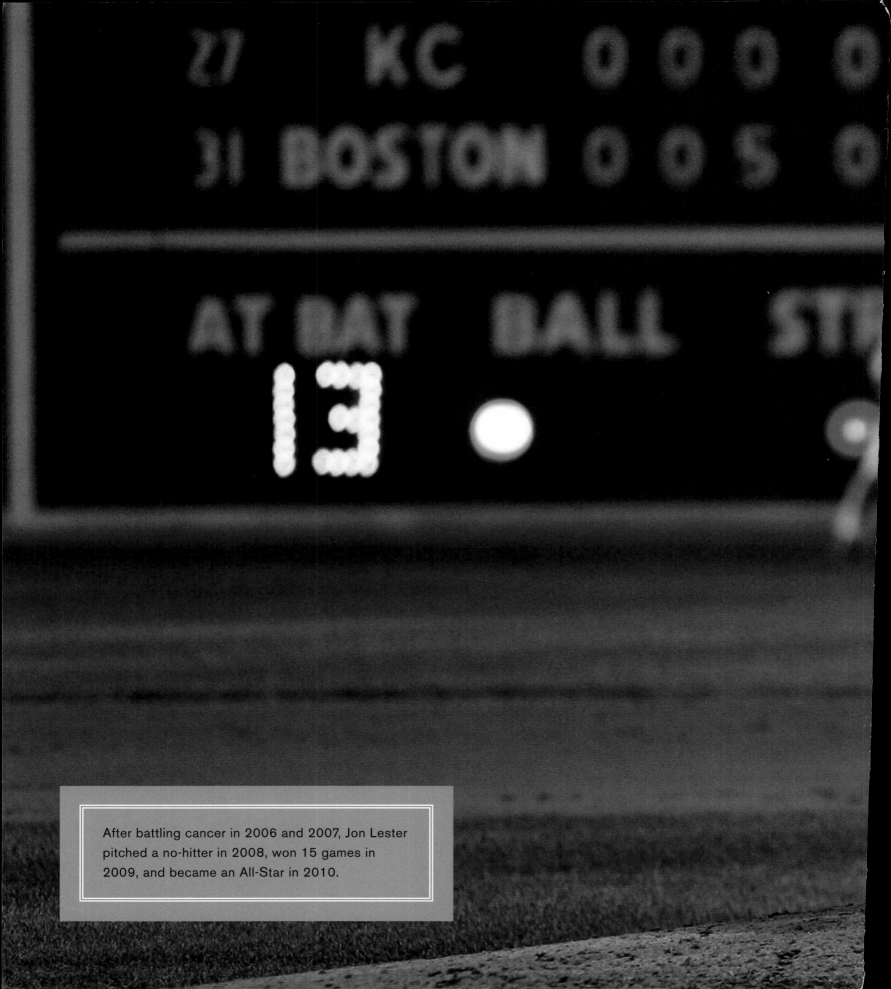

After battling cancer in 2006 and 2007, Jon Lester pitched a no-hitter in 2008, won 15 games in 2009, and became an All-Star in 2010.

JON LESTER

DUSTIN PEDROIA

Although Boston missed the playoffs in 2010, Dustin Pedroia (opposite) and Victor Martinez (right) helped the Sox assemble a winning record for the 13th straight season.

VICTOR MARTINEZ

2008 season included some newsworthy controversy. Moody slugger Manny Ramirez, who seemed to be playing at half-speed early in the year, was traded to the Los Angeles Dodgers in a midseason move that disappointed many Sox fans.

The Red Sox won 95 games in 2009 to reach the playoffs again, but this time, they were quickly eliminated by the Angels in the first round. In 2010 and 2011, the Sox put together stellar records but just missed the postseason. Still, Boston fans remained confident about their club's future. With Beckett and lefty Jon Lester leading the pitching corps and Pedroia, Youkilis, and new outfielder Carl Crawford keying the offense, the Red Sox appeared to be loaded with talent for seasons to come.

For more than 100 years, the Boston Red Sox have given their faithful fans a colorful history full of championship victories, heartbreaking defeats, curses, and even a green monster. More than just the hometown team, the Red Sox have become a rooting obsession for sports fans throughout New England, who proudly proclaim themselves to be citizens of "Red Sox Nation."

INDEX